RUNNING SMARTER

21 RUNNING HABITS FOR FASTER TIMES AND FEWER INJURIES

VON COLLINS

Running just might be the world's most efficient workout. It is a natural movement that nearly everyone can do. Unlike cycling or swimming, it doesn't require expensive equipment or going to a particular facility. It requires successful coordination of many muscle groups, band burns serious calories. And it takes full advantage of an athlete's cardiovascular system, allowing for growth in conditioning.

Whether you are a competitive runner or a weekend jogger, running can provide workouts that race the heart, tone the muscles, and relax the mind. It is a worldwide sport and a favorite pastime with people of all types and nationalities

But it is not perfect.

Runners can face the same obstacles as athletes in any other sport. They hit plateaus in their training, causing stagnation in race times or peak distances. They can injure themselves with overuse and non-contact injuries, sometimes severely. Unlike swimming, yoga, or cycling, running has a reputation of wearing out the body -- particularly the knees and legs -- before the runner is ready to hang up the shoes.

My goal in writing this book is to help you learn 21 simple habits that can elongate your running career, and can help you break through to new personal records if you are a competitive runner. It is a mix of proven rules from the sports science world and truisms from the seasoned runners I have trained with over the years.

As you train, I want you to balance three important things. The first is for you to experience the true joy of running. The sun in your face, running through beautiful and serene places, and enjoying the endorphin high that you often get after a quality workout.

The second is consistent improvement. It is a great feeling to go for a run, and realize you can do it either easier or faster than you could just a couple weeks before. This feeling creates a cycle -- a desire to keep improving, so your runs can be faster, longer, or just more comfortable to do. All the while, you will notice changes in your body that will likely be welcomed -- fat burning off, muscles becoming toned, and more.

The third is to run without injury. Injuries are some of the most disappointing things that a runner can experience, because they disrupt your training, cause discomfort (sometimes major), and set your fitness back. If you can avoid injury, you have won half the battle. Fortunately, there are things you can do to reduce the odds of incurring an injury as a runner.

This guide will help you develop 21 running habits for achieving faster times and avoiding injuries, and ultimately enjoying the sport of running in ways that so many before you have.

RELATED RESOURCES

As you dive into this book, I want to give you some additional, related resources that may help you in your fitness and racing journey. All of my books can be found on Amazon.

<u>30 Essential Running Workouts, 30 Minutes or Less.</u> Time-strapped? This book provides 30 excellent running and cross-training workouts that help you make the most of your training time.

<u>Fit Foods: 21 Nutrition Rules for Getting More From Your Training, Runs, and Workouts</u>. Nutrition is a secret weapon of anyone who is training or trying to get more fit. This guide breaks it down in laymen's terms.

<u>Your First Triathlon Guide: 100 Days to Your First Triathlon</u>. For total body conditioning, and a great balance of cardio and muscular fitness, there is no better sport than triathlon. I give you the step-by-step on how you can enjoy the sport.

Finally, my email subscribers are the first to hear about the best gear and equipment deals, as well as new content that might be helpful. I don't send many emails, so don't worry – I won't clutter your inbox! <u>You can sign up here.</u>

TABLE OF CONTENTS

1. Practice Periodization

My first tip is all about having peak seasons and offseasons. Running is meant to be something that you throttle up and throttle down within the course of a life, a year, or even a season. It is very important to realize that you can't perform at 100% effort indefinitely. Actually, you can't perform at your peak fitness for more than a couple of months at a time. Knowing this is the first step in a healthy flow and tempo for your runner's body.

Unfortunately, many runners out there are trying to achieve some consistency by getting out every single day and sometimes doing the exact same thing day-in and day-out. This doesn't work, because humans are so amazingly adaptable that they will eventually gain very little benefit from doing exactly the same thing day after day. Your body will become efficient, whether you want it to or not. On the contrary: by doing getting into a rut and doing the same workout for years on end, runners get sick, deal with aches, pain, injury, or burnout. When you induce yourself with too much lactic acid from high-intensity training, your aerobic enzymes will start getting destroyed, you'll fatigue your muscle fibers, and your endocrine system will beg you to rest.

In order to get faster times, longer distances, and avoid injuries, you have to practice periodization. The purpose of periodization is to change the stimulus but at the same time aim it towards a peak season. Thus, you want to work hard enough so that you 'break yourself down' in order to recover more strongly than before. Essentially, that is really what any workout is -- putting your body under stress, so that it uses its adaptability to rebuild itself just a little strong than it was the day before.

If you're more of a beginner runner, keep things simple. Take an offseason after every intense running season/event and wipe the slate clean. This way, you will create good physical and mental balance that will payoff in the form of fewer injuries and better focus. This doesn't mean sitting on your couch all day long. During your offseasons, do some light cross training or have some low-impact activity; this will give your endocrine system a well-deserved break as well as let your muscles heal and recover. Many runners choose yoga, but do whatever gets you excited. Then, slowly and gradually come back with easy aerobic, slow-paced running to build back up and introduce some intensity until you're able to get back and ultimately achieve even better results than before. When doing this, you super-compensate and reach periods in your season when you're stronger and better than at any other given time.

If you're more of a seasoned runner, you can use periodization to create a performance-achieving schedule. Designing a well-thought plan that uses the concept of periodization will support you break down your big goal into smaller cycles. Periodization helps you reach your peak performance when you need it the most. It will build you up through different periods, focusing on different aspects of your training and then getting you to peak performance exactly when you need it. It does that by altering the number of miles you're putting in or how intensely you're working and it keeps everything in balance.

Each cycle has its specific purpose. The most used method involves a three cycle periodization with a microcycle, a mesocycle, and a macrocycle. During microcycles (that can last from a couple of days to a couple of weeks) repeat your workout pattern (for example a long run, an uphill run, a couple of easy runs, a lactate turn point run, a VO2max training, and a rest day) on and on again until the end of the cycle. The mesocycle can last from a few weeks to a few months and is a training block consisting of multiple microcycles that focus on one or two training types: speed, distance, VO2max, endurance, power, strength, or a combo. The macrocycle has a moderate to a long-term goal and usually lasts from several months to an entire year. Macrocycles are made of many mesocycles and focus on accomplishing a big goal like finishing a marathon, getting good results in a tough race, or setting a new PR in an important race.

The most important thing to do is to mix and match your peak and off seasons according to your physical activity level, the type of running that you practice and your running goals. Also, if you're getting into a periodization cycle scheme, choose and combine your trainings in order to improve the aspects you're not very good at (strength, speed, length, and so on), as well as letting your body actively gradually rebuild before getting back into that peak season.

2. LEARN HOW TO BREATHE CORRECTLY

When I was first getting in to running, I had a coach ask me if I had worked on my breathing. Breathing? I thought running was all about putting one foot in front of the other.

Most of us think that breathing is an innate skill we possess. Surely, we do not need any training on how to do it! Yes, breathing is technically an involuntary action that your body takes, but knowing how to control your breathing is useful in everything from relaxing to swimming to our running topic.

When running becomes a habit and you don't know how to properly breathe, you risk not getting the optimal amount of oxygen in your blood. You will find yourself getting tired quickly and not give it all you've got. In order to improve your running, one key secret is learning how to breathe for performance.

Breathing correctly while you're running is very important. It will help you enhance your physical resistance, run faster and longer without quickly feeling exhausted. Proper breathing also improves blood circulation, especially in the legs; muscle mass grows and the cramps disappear.

Running can make you feel like you're out of breath. A correct breathing technique will help you solve this problem.

The feeling of running out of breath is due to the intensity of the effort you make when you run. Imagine that your body relies on oxygen in order to function. When you run, your lungs have to "work" a lot more to absorb the oxygen from the air and send it to your muscles in order to keep them moving. The faster you run, trying to exceed your limits, the more you can feel like you lack air. This kind of oxygen debt can become more of a limiting factor than weak leg muscles or poor running form.

Sometimes, however, it's possible that the feeling of airlessness also occurs because of poor breathing, either breathing too fast or too slow. In fact, breathing is essential for running like a pro. Properly breathing while you run can greatly improve your resistance and you will be able to go longer distances without getting tired and feeling the effort as a burden. Next, we'll present some breathing techniques that will help your body supply oxygen more effectively to your muscles so that you feel comfortable, run faster, longer, and avoid injuries.

Proper breathing has some simple but very important rules that make running easier and more efficient.

Breathe through both your mouth and nose.

Although it's natural to breathe through your nose, when you run, it's actually recommended to breathe through your mouth and nose. This way, you'll be able to inhale more oxygen and exhale more carbon dioxide. Thus, your muscles will receive a sufficient amount of oxygen. You are also likely to breath deeply if you breathe through your mouth, and that brings us to our next point.

Learn to breathe as deeply as possible

When you run, you should do stomach breathing (aka diaphragmatic, abdominal, or belly breathing), not chest breathing. This is the only way you'll be able to supplement the amount of oxygen your body needs to sustain the physical effort. You can practice stomach breathing when you lie down in bed:

relax, inhale deeply and exhale gently, calmly. You should notice how your abdomen goes up and down.

The respiratory rhythm is crucial

And that's because it helps you sustain the effort. Rhythmic breathing was a key principle that the running coach, who I referred to at the beginning of this chapter, tried to teach me.

A good breathing rhythm creates the foundation for successful long-term running. Therefore, you should inhale and exhale at a constant pace no matter how fast or slow you run. Here's a good method that will help you pace your breath: count a few steps while you're running (two to three steps) and then inhale; after the next two to three steps, exhale. And so on. Work on expanding your breathing ability over time. If you could do one breathing cycle every 4 steps before, work to improve that to every 6 steps over time. This will make your cardiovascular system more efficient in the long run (no pun intended).

Some coaches suggest that the ideal breathing rhythm for runners is an inhale for three steps, and then an exhale for two. The longer inhale encourages deep, full breathing. And the odd number of steps per full breathing stroke means that your breathing is not locked in to a left foot / right foot habit, which could help with balancing your alignmnet.

If you want to learn to control your breathing, consider engaging in yoga (tip #11).

Short, deep breaths for running faster

Breathing deeply is important to bring as much oxygen as possible to your body. However, if you have long, deep breaths, you won't be able to increase your speed. For this reason, if you are sprinting, you should combine long, deep breathing with short, deep breathing so that your body receives enough oxygen. You can try to run faster while breathing briefly and deeply and when you get tired, slow down the pace and use long, deep breathing. As you get more comfortable manipulating your breathing, by all means try to extend the cycle to get another stride or two out of each breath. But don't go so far as to breath really deep and long, you want to focus on keeping new oxygen in your blood.

3. INCORPORATE UPHILL RUNS

Uphill training runs are a secret weapon of some of the best 5K and 10K runners out there. If you live in a hilly area, then an uphill training day comes with the turf. If you live in the flat land, you will need to seek out a hill -- but it will be worth it.

Running on a treadmill set to incline is always an option as well, if running indoors is your thing.

Uphill running should be included in your training regularly. Not only does it burn more calories in a shorter period of time than running on flats, but it significantly increases speed, resistance, overall performance, and helps you avoid injuries.

When run uphill, you use your major leg muscles (quads and hamstrings) much more than when you're running on flat ground. Even if it's a bit more difficult, take a step further in overcoming your limitations, as stronger muscles mean increased running speed, improved metabolism, and enhanced calorie burning.

When running uphill, your legs build lactic acid more quickly, causing fatigue. You involuntarily pass some of the efforts on to the upper part of your body, especially to your arms. This translates into a stronger trunk and a more pleasant posture. Of course, you should also use your arms when running on flat terrain, and it's absolutely necessary to move them continuously, never keep them stiff.

Uphill running helps you reduce the risk of getting injured. How? The explanation is pretty simple: you use your leg muscles more intensely, thus you're strengthening them and reducing the risk of dealing with the annoying runner's knee. You are also working important supporting muscles in a way that you wouldn't if you just go for the same flat run every day.

This type of workout will improve endurance, so you're going to be able to run faster and longer. Plus, it uses the same muscles as if you were sprinting; another reason why you'll manage to run longer and faster.

Finally, uphill running is a very time-effective training method. When you're working against gravity, you'll obviously get more calories burned, so you can get the muscular work in 20 minutes that it would perhaps take 40 minutes to get on flat ground. Uphill running is a great alternative if time is a premium and you don't have enough of it for a long run.

Here are some helpful tips to master uphill running:

Keep your hips forward. Many folks that are getting into uphill running tend to bent at the hips and lean into the hill a tad too much. Being in this position takes a lot of stress into your back. If you stay tall, keep your chest up and hips forward, you'll run faster up the hill and you'll feel better afterwards as well.

Keep your cadence high. On flat ground, you usually have a really great cadence, yet when you go up a slope, you tend to slow down significantly. What you want to avoid is getting to a point where you're slowing up the hill. It will take a lot of energy for you to do that, so you'll keep your cadence as high as it is on flat ground. Shorten your stride, and get in to a nice, steady tempo. Taking short steps will help you maintain a high cadence.

Relax your ankles. This will take a ton of stress out of your calves. As you go up the hill, it takes a bunch of effort for your calves to get you up to the top. Therefore, if you relax your ankles and let your heels 'kiss' the ground, every time that you're taking a step, your calves won't flare up on you.

Be careful on the downhills. If you run uphill, sooner or later you have to run downhill. Unlike uphill running, downhill running has few health benefits. In fact, it can really hurt your knees. Take it easy going downhill, and perhaps even walk. There is no benefit from running fast downhill. The point of running downhill is simply to get back down safely. Make sure your feet are striking the ground as lightly as possible, and again, shorten your stride.

4. WORK ON YOUR RUNNING POSTURE

We have all watched the end of running races. Perhaps you were cheering on a friend or family member, or maybe you had finished and were resting while watching other runners finish. You probably noticed that there are dozens of variations of running posture. Some look healthy and productive. Others look like they can't be good on the knees, hips, and back.

The reason why you want to work towards a proper running posture is to run faster, more efficiently, and reduce the risk of injury. Here are some key points that will help you improve your posture when you're running.

The ideal running form

What you have to look for in an ideal form is a tall, elongated body from the head down to the toes. There's generally a natural forward lean that comes from the ankle. Focus on maintaining this lean rather than breaking from the hips or collapsing in the chest - this often happens with fatigue. Aim to have relaxed shoulders and arms. Your arms should be at 90 degrees at the height of your hips. Hands should be relaxed as well, with loose fingers. This all allows you to maximize your lung capacity, to breathe from the abdomen rather than superficially breathing from the chest. Focus on having a short, quick stride with a fast turnover of the feet; don't try to overreach or over lengthen each stride. The feet should fall directly under your body with each stride and, preferably, aim for a midfoot strike.

Have someone video you running at various speeds. Look at your form, and be sure your feet are under you, that your body lean looks natural and comfortable, and that your joints are aligned in a way that looks friction-and-hitch-free.

In detail

Head. Keep your head straight, as an extension of your spine, in order to breathe easily. Don't move it back or bring it to the chest, because your neck will feel tense. Keep your face and jaw muscles relaxed. If it's sunny outside, wear sunglasses; otherwise, you will end up with a headache. If you are running in cold weather, consider a neck gaiter and running hat to keep warm. If you get cold, you might unknowingly modify how you hold your head which affects your alignment.

Shoulders. Without even realizing, you can end up keeping your shoulders hunched while you run. This posture, besides making breathing difficult, also adds a lot of pressure to your knees and lower back. Roll your shoulders, un-hunch them, and check their form several times during a run.

Arms. Your arms should never be lower than your waist, but also not up at your chest either. In order to increase your speed, move your arms in the same rhythm as your feet and keep them at a comfortable 90 degree angle. If your arms are swinging loosely and comfortably, you are more likely to also keep your shoulders relaxed. One thing leads to another.

Hands. Keeping your fists contracted will tense your arm and shoulder muscles and sometimes can even lead to pain. Not to mention that it will make you look like a grumpy, angry runner, and you are then expending energy on something not critical to your running. Open your hands and keep your palms and fingers relaxed. When you're running at a moderate pace, don't lift your palms higher than your sternum.

Hips and abs. Many runners deal with lower back pain because they don't keep their abs tight when they're running. Tightening your abs will help your pelvis and lumbar area be steady and stable while you're moving.

Feet. In order to increase your speed and strength, use your midfoot and toes rather than your heels. Your feet have to be aligned with your knees and chest whenever they hit the ground. A smooth landing is also essential -- try to focus on having your entire foot bottom touch the ground during each stride. If only the inside or outside of your foot makes contact with the ground, you are likely misaligning the rest of your leg. Injuries will follow.

Shortening your running stride is a good way to move your foot strike to the midfoot rather than the heel.

Once you become more aware of proper running form, don't force any abrupt changes, as this can also lead to injury. Slowly, gradually work towards the ideal posture.

I will note again the value of having a friend video you while running. This is much easier now than it was 10 years ago, with a smartphone in everyone's pocket. Study your running gait -- is it symmetrical? Do you lean forward at the ankle? Is your foot striking the ground properly? Do you look relaxed? Are your arms swinging comfortably, or are you fighting them?

5. Warm-up Properly

A proper warm-up is a time-tested rule for preparing for a safe and effective run. Two main roles of the warm-up include helping get proper blood flow to the connective membranes in your joints, and increasing flexibility in your leg muscles, both of which will help you run more comfortably and prevent injury. Let's take a deeper look into the warm-up benefits. Here are some of them:

· Dilates blood vessels, ensuring an increased blood flow and oxygen to the muscles. This allows you to produce more energy;
· Increases muscle temperature for better flexibility;
· Slightly increases the heart rate, so the heart won't have to deal with sudden stress once you enhance the running intensity;
· Stimulates the activity of the central nervous system. Here is where you hold all the motor and movement patterns that you've learned from previous experiences. By allowing the central nervous system time to activate, it lets you do things such as move quicker, create more strength, and perform physical activity in a more skilful manner;
· Lubricates the joints. Your joints lubricate through movement, and blood flow increases in the all-important membranes that connect the pieces of your joint. As you start at a low intensity and gradually build up, the movement within the joints allows synovial fluid to flow into them and make sure that they can lubricate properly. This decreases the risk of any damage occurring throughout the running session;

- Adjusts the enzymes and hormones that are responsible for energy production. Your body is set up for optimal energy production when you first start to exercise. Thus, warming up allows you to perform at a higher level;
- Decreases post-workout muscle soreness. Yes, we're talking about that annoying muscle soreness that you sometimes experience 24 to 48 hours after running.

What if you skip the warm-up?

If you skip a warm-up, there is a shock to your system on many levels which can be detrimental to your workout. During the warm-up, there is a redistribution of blood flow; you need blood flowing through the muscles so they get activated. Besides oxygen, blood also carries nutrients that allow the muscles to keep contracting. If you don't have adequate blood flow, then you move to your anaerobic system which may cause you to struggle with premature fatigue. Also, if you don't do your warm-up properly, your heart can actually change the way in which it contracts and this is something unhealthy for you. Finally, if you immediately begin working out with intensity, there is a chance of damaging your cold joints.

Warm-up exercises: types and length

Before running, you should warm-up for about 5-10 minutes; although stretching exercises are great for increasing the body's flexibility, don't start with them, because your muscles are not warmed up yet, thus not able to handle stretching painlessly. Start with light aerobic exercises, such as walking, light jogging, cycling, some easy lunges, or a few minutes on the stationary bike. A combination of light aerobic moves (which target the entire body, not just the legs) and some stretching exercises afterward is ideal.

For example, you can start with 30 seconds of jumping jacks; this exercise targets the arms, legs, abs, and glutes. After that, you can continue with some easy walking. If you choose to do it on a treadmill, make sure not to neglect your arms; move them in the same rhythm as your legs. Next, continue walking and, simultaneously, do some torso twists to warm-up the abdominal muscles. Leg swings, calf stretches, and butt kicks are other awesome moves for warming up your lower body.

Many runners begin their runs with an easy 3-5 minutes of jogging, then stop and stretch, and then resume their run at more of a training pace. That works too, and allows you to get out on the trail or path right away.

6. COOL DOWN PROPERLY

Have you ever finished running or working out, then just sat down and started to feel a little light-headed, had some cramping muscles, and just didn't feel so well? Or maybe you noticed how, an hour after great workout, your legs were seizing up and getting stiffer by the minute?

The cool down is an important part of any workout, in order to ease your body in to a good resting -- and rejuvinative -- state. If you want to stay healthy, run your fastest times, reach your fullest potential, and stay away from injuries, you should be always cool down properly. It may seem like a little thing, but that's exactly what will set you apart from folks who just hammer the running session and skip the cool-down.

The purpose of a cool down is to get your body back to a resting state, and one that will allow it to make the necessary repairs from the workout you just did. A proper cool down brings the heart rate back to normal by gradually decreasing your breathing rate. It improves your recovery by preventing blood pooling in the veins which causes a lot of swelling in your muscles. It also re-circulates your blood, helps to rid those by-products, and brings nutrient-dense blood back through your muscles.

Cooling down also helps you avoid a sudden drop in blood pressure that can cause fainting. A good recommendation for the time of your cool-down is about 5 - 10 minutes, which should be supplemented by beginning to hydrate and gradually refill your body with electrolytes.

Here are some examples of cooling down.

Immediately after a running session or a race, **brisk walk or jog very easily** in order to slowly bring back your breathing rate to normal levels. Your stride should be short - nearly a shuffle. If you had been monitoring your power, speed, or heart rate, don't worry about that now. Just go easy.

Also, as part of a cool-down, you want to carefully integrate into static stretches. Stretching after a workout is a great opportunity to expand your muscle length and build range-of-motion. Because your muscles are warm after workout out, they are more elastic. As a result, the stretches you do during this time can actually help reset your muscles in a more flexible state, if done consistently.

These are some static stretches (each of these should be held about 30 seconds to a minute, depending on your tolerance) every runner should do:

Hip flexor stretch. The hip flexor is a very commonly tight muscle on runners and a lot of that has to do with you sitting most of the day. When it's tight, this muscle limits your ability to get your leg behind you, which then prevents you from running faster or from running with proper form. So the way that you have to stretch it is in a half kneeling position. The key thing is to make sure that you don't arch your back when you stretch. And this is because that would stretch your back out, not the muscle. So start in this position, with your knee underneath your hips, and the first thing you want to do is to round your lower back out. Most of you will feel a stretch on the front side of the leg when you do this; that's the area that you want to stretch. For those of you who don't feel a stretch yet, you can move a bit forward without letting your back arch.

Hip flexor stretch modifier. If you can't easily get into the kneeling position, there is a standing modified version that you can do. You simply have to start in shoulder width apart in split stance and stretch your muscle. Again, make sure that you're not arching your back as you do this stretch. Round your lower back out until you feel a stretch along the front side of your leg. If you need more of a stretch, then you can raise your hand, reach up and across your body until you feel the stretch engage.

Gastrocnemius and soleus stretch. Both of these muscles (gastrocnemius and soleus) make up your calf muscle, yet they are totally separate muscles that need to be stretched individually. In order to stretch the gastrocnemius, start in shoulder width apart in split stance; make sure that your toes are pointed straight forward and that you keep your back heel on the ground. Lean forward, keeping the knee of the leg that's behind straight. You should feel the stretching at the back of your knee. Then, switch to the soleus stretch. Bend the knee and drop straight down from that position. You should feel this stretch a little lower in your calf, which is where your muscle attaches.

7. TAKE HYDRATION SERIOUSLY

Hydration has a profound influence on your performance. Every experienced runner, cyclist, or triathlete has a story of "bonking" in a race -- not because they weren't trained properly, but because they lacked proper hydration on race day.

Our bodies are made up of 50% to 70% water, which is vital for every chemical reaction in our body. We need plenty of fluids in order to help the nutrients' transport, support the cellular enzymatic activity, digestion, toxins and waste removal, brain functioning support, as well as for a good mood, enhanced energy levels, and focus.

When we run, we also lose some key electrolytes (mainly sodium) through our sweat. In our body, electrolytes control all of the electrical impulses and stimuli such as brain functioning, heart beating, and muscle firing - all of these are essential for runners. And, besides water, you need to bring in some kind of hydration product that contains those electrolytes.

The average person loses about 1 liter of water during an hour of exercise, according to Active.com. And according to studies by the NIH, your exact water loss during a workout may be more than that, depending on the outside temperature, humidity level, and of course exertion level.

As a rule of thumb, it's extremely important for you to be well hydrated before, during, and after a running session or a race.

Dehydration often leads to fatigue, muscle cramps, decreased ability to coordinate movements.

How to tell if you're dehydrated?

There are a few common signs you can look for:

· headaches

· nausea

· dry mouth

· increased body temperature

· increased heart rate

· dizziness

· fatigue

· less clarity of mind

How to stay hydrated

Here are some things to consider when building your hydration plan.

Take the sweat test. Although this is not the most accurate way of telling how much sodium you're losing, it's still an awesome step to start with. The easiest way to do it is to weight yourself before you go for a run. Ideally, this run should take about 1 hour in warm (or hot), humid conditions. If you live in a colder area, bundle up and put some layers on. Then weigh yourself again when you return from the run and see the difference. If you've lost about 1/2 pound, you're considered a light to moderate sweater. If you're in the 3 to 4 pounds range, you're considered a heavy sweater. Therefore, you'll get an idea of how much water weight you're losing.

Search for a hydration product. Find something that works for you, tastes well, it's high in sodium and low in sugar. Make sure it's a product that you'll be able to easily carry with you.

Sports drinks are created to offer you an optimal combination of water, electrolytes, and other substances you need during running. There are several types of hydration products:

· *Hypotonic* . They contain a small number of carbohydrates (usually less than 4%). This is lower than blood plasma concentration and is therefore easily assimilated and digested.

· *Isotonic*. They contain between 4-8% carbohydrates as well as some electrolytes. The concentration is similar to that of plasma in the blood, thus they're a better choice to replace fluids quickly during long-distance runs.

· *Hypertonic*. They contain a higher carbohydrate concentration (over 8%), but don't have electrolytes, and are sometimes used to restore glycogen stores after training. They can also be used during challenging races, but should be combined with isotonic beverages to ensure sodium intake.

Map out the course and plan accordingly. This way, you'll be able to adjust your hydration fluid consumption according to the temperature, humidity, and so on. If there's going to be a hot, humid day, increase your sodium intake and keep your body cool. On a cooler day, you might be able to get away with drinking a little less. Also, know where all the aid stations are and what they have on the course. Plan out if you'll wear a hydration pack, a handheld bottle, or anything else.

Other key recommendations to stay hydrated. Don't wait until you get thirsty; drink liquids regularly before, during, and after you run. Also, make sure to drink small fluid amounts frequently and get your body used with that.

Many athletes falsely think that hydration is really only about drinking water during or after a run. It is really about a lifestyle, though. A person who stays well-hydrated throughout the week is more likely to have proper hydration on their runs. Like a student taking a test, it is best to prepare continuously rather than cram right before the big event.

The night before a long run or a race, drink plenty of water and avoid more than a drink or so of alcohol. If you are running in a race like a 10K or half marathon, take a drink of water at every place it is offered along the course. Even if you don't feel thirsty yet and hate to slow down to grab the water cup, there is a very good chance you have been sweating and could use the hydration. The 3-5 seconds you lose by grabbing a gulp of water will probably be more than made up by the pace you are able to sustain later in the run.

8. SCHEDULE RECOVERY TIME

To be more specific, focus on recovery weeks. A recovery week is simply a week when you lower the volume, lower your runs' length, intensity, and allow your body some well-deserved time to regenerate from the last weeks of hard work.

If the week happens to be following an A-Race or an intense season of running, then the right recovery week may well be doing nothing at all.

Recovery is defined as restoring your performance capacity after an intense period of running. It's very important and has to be seen as putting yourself into a 'recharging mode' after some significant physical effort. It's essential for every runner to understand and accept that continuous progress will inevitably require some stagnation phases or even some performance-reduction temporary phases.

'Recharging' methods aim at speeding up recovery, preventing injuries, and increasing your performance capacity. Fatigue can be physical and mental, thus recovery has to address both of these aspects. So, the main reason why you need recovery weeks is actually because that's the time when you're going to see all the gains that you've been putting in, all that hard work, and you'll finally allow your body to grow stronger and get faster. After a recovery week, you'll come back stronger, faster, and be able to continue your build cycle.

How to do a recovery week

Basically, if we are talking about the type of recovery week that may happen mid-season, you need to take about 30% to 40% off the volume of running that you did the past weeks. So whatever number of miles that you did, take off 30% to 40% off that. If you did a super long run in the previous week, increase the percentage; take 30% to 50% off of it and stick to that during your recovery week.

Another key is to lower the overall intensity of your runs. This might seem counter-intuitive if you are trying to get faster, but it all goes with the periodization concept I wrote about earlier. If you are constantly going all out, there is no variety in your conditioning. Keep doing a run or two that crank up your intensity intensity, but the overall mantra for the recovery week should be lowering the intensity of your runs and giving your body time to rest and recharge.

A good analogy for recovery weeks is climbing a tall mountain. People who conquer high peaks always climb up a little bit then they stop and give their body time to acclimate to that different weather and new altitude. That's because the human body needs time to adapt. The same thing applies for running: as you're increasing the volume, length, and intensity of your runs, you need time to adapt to that new training and to improve even further from that point.

You have several options for recovery weeks: for example, you can do a 3-week running cycle, a 4-week running cycle (the most common one), or a 5-week running cycle. The most recommended one and the one that suits most runners is the 4-week running cycle. This involves doing three weeks in a row of building up your volume, intensity, and length; on the fourth week, focus on the recovery where you lower the volume, intensity, and length. The 3-week running cycle is great for those of you who are very prone to injury, illness or overtraining. It's also suitable for folks who're just coming back into running. For this, you have only two weeks of build and then a recovery one. The 5-week running cycle (four weeks of build and one of recovery) is for people who're very experienced, used to running a lot of miles, and have proven their ability to do that without getting injured.

Don't forget about sprinkling "recovery runs" in throughout your season, even when training is in full force. For a typical week, a good rule of thumb is that half of your runs should be of the recovery variety -- LSD (long, slow distance) to use an 80s term. So, if you are doing 5 runs per week, 2-3 should be very intentional and intense training runs, while 2-3 should be easier recovery runs.

Back to recovery weeks, you will be amazed how well they work. Some of the best races I've run have been after taking a week to really throttle down the runs or even cease for a few days altogther. I always come back stronger. In a nutshell, make sure you're adding recovery weeks into your training so you can keep getting stronger, faster, and enjoy running.

9. AVOID CONCRETE OR PAVER SURFACES

Many people focus their running habits on important things like the training plan, stretching, nutrition, and intensity. But an overlooked part of staying healthy and injury-free is finding a running surface that doesn't beat your body up. Over time, seeking out a good surface will pay dividends.

Depending on the surface that you run on, your training can be more effective or, if you don't make a good choice, more dangerous. On the long-term, the running surface can negatively affect your physical health.

As someone who enjoys running and wants to prevent injuries, you should be aware that not all surfaces are great to run on. For example, concrete or paver surfaces are not an ideal choice. When running on this kind of surfaces your body uses more force compared to the force used when running on grass, sand, or normal jogging tracks. Thus, your knees are more impacted when dealing with hard surfaces.

As a rule of thumb, concrete or paver surfaces should be avoided at all costs. Many runners who've made that mistake eventually struggle with pain or injuries. Due to these surfaces' roughness, all the force that you use to 'hit the ground' comes back on you, damaging your joints, ligaments, and putting way too much pressure on your spine. Your body simply can't take that much stress. Not to mention falling on such surfaces, that can have extremely unpleasant outcomes.

The best surface to run on is often a specially-built, soft running track. However, if you don't have any of these in your nearby area, there are still some running-friendly options to consider. For example, thick grass and dirt are nice picks. They can successfully soak up the impact of your feet against the soil. Anyway, practice some basic caution when running on high grass, as there can be hidden obstacles or holes you can encounter along the way. Sand is an awesome, injury-free choice if you also want to burn more calories while you run. As your feet are slightly sinking in it, you will need to put more effort than on another surface.

According to Runner's World Magazine, the best surfaces to run on for knee and joint health, in order, are below. Try to focus on the top six to maintain long-term knee and joint health.

Best Surfaces

- Grass
- Woodland trails
- Dirt trails
- Cinder
- Synthetic track
- Treadmill

Worst Surfaces

- Asphalt
- Sand
- Concrete
- Snow and ice (see our next tip)

10. RUN SAFELY IN WINTER

It's important to adapt your running style according to the season. For many runners, winter is perhaps the most difficult season to maintain mileage and intensity. Fortunately, it is often the time of year when an offseason or cross-training phase is called for so the need for high mileage is less, but you still want to run outside when you can.

You shouldn't put running on pause during winter, but always take into account the weather conditions. One split-second slip on an icy road could set your training back for months. I certainly do not want to see that happen to you.

For outdoor runners in northern climates, winter is not the ideal season to suddenly increase your distance or your speed, as it takes more physical effort and energy running on snow and in low temperatures. Therefore, it will be a bit challenging to keep up with your current miles. While progress requires pushing your limits, a harsh winter isn't the perfect setting for that. Freezing weather and ice are factors that can lead to muscle stretches or fractures, so you have to focus more on being cautious than to reach a big milestone.

While running on hard pack snow can be a good experience, running on ice should be avoided altogether. The risk of falling, thus getting injured is highly increased, so stick to those ice-free areas. I know of many runners in my immediate circles who suffered major injury because of a patch of ice. Twisted knees, injured hips, fractured wrists or shoulders (from trying to break the fall), and injured vertebrae tend to be the more common ice-related inuries.

Make a list with some nearby tracks or trails that are constantly taken care of, so there's no ice along your way. It might involve a brief commute, but it will be worth it. Don't worry if there's a bit of snow on the ground. As opposed to ice, snow provides adhesion, thus it's much safer and beneficial as long as you wear proper footwear.

Winter running attire

In winter, you have to dress properly when you go out for a run. Use socks that are warm, able to absorb sweat and make sure you have enough space for fitting them in your running shoes. Go for a not-too-tight, not-too-loose pair of socks. You can purchase a pair of running shoes that run half a size bigger than you normally wear in order to easily fit that pair of thick socks. Using suitable footwear and socks is essential to avoid frostbite or blood circulation problems. Any cold weather veteran knows that having a little bit of breathing room inside a shoe or boot is the key to the foot staying warm. Tighter is not good in cold conditions.

Another rule of thumb of running in winter is layering. For your lower body, you can wear a wicking base layer, an insulating layer, and a windproof/waterproof layer. Regarding the lower body, tights and running pants are a great choice. A thermal hat will do an amazing job of protecting your head, while a neck gaiter or bandana will keep your neck warm. Don't forget about the gloves or mittens. Using multiple layers of clothes will help you move freely without freezing. The cold season is also the time when you have to pay special attention to your underwear. Opt for items that are comfortable and offer protection against cold.

Avoid cotton base layers, as it tends to lose its insulative properties quickly once it absorbs water. Instead, always opt for a wool or synthetic base. They can retain more of their insulation qualities even after getting somewhat wet.

Win the fight against wind-caused dehydration

Wind can be very dangerous when you run in winter, as it can easily dehydrate you. It is recommended to run with the wind blowing from the front and return home with the wind blowing from your back. Even if outside is cold and you don't really feel thirsty, try to drink as many liquids as you can. Hot drinks, especially teas are a good choice and can be carried in a thermally insulated bottle.

Protect your skin

When running in winter, don't forget to use a moisturizer that also provides sun protection. You will thus avoid dehydration and your skin won't turn red. Use a high-quality moisturizer and apply it abundantly, especially on your cheeks and nose, the areas that are most exposed during running.

11. Inject yoga or pilates into your plan

While running might be one of the world's oldest forms of exercise, yoga isn't far behind. People have been doing it for nearly 5,000 years, and for good reason. Pilates, related in that it is all about controlled body movements, has been around for well over a century as well. There's no secret that yoga and Pilates help you enhance your overall bodily functioning.

It is very important for runners to have a strong core which, biomechanically speaking is like an anchor of the running technique. When your core is not strong enough, your running technique and form tend to get out of control as soon as you get tired; this can cause those unpleasant, stress-related injuries. By including yoga and Pilates 2 -3 times a week into your workout routine, you'll strengthen your core, as well as every other part of your body and enjoy a physical and mental improvement.

Yoga benefits for runners

Yoga is extremely effective for running aficionados as it involves dynamic stretches of those muscles that are tired, stressed, overworked, or shortened by overuse. All of this results in a muscle imbalance that can lead to injury. Therefore, you want to focus on stretching and stabilizing key areas in order to overcome physical challenges.

Yoga Journal, the top popular authority on practicing yoga, notes several benefits of yoga for runners. Among them are reduced muscle rigidity, improved range-of-motion, and a more balanced physique which can result in fewer "domino-effect" injuries. That sore knee you have been feeling? I might be due to your misaligned back, which is really due to your weak core. It all links together, and when done right, yoga can correct many of the root cause issues.

When you run, your calves, hips, hamstrings, knees, quads, and ankles are intensely working. If they're not properly stretched, they'll either start recruiting help from different muscles that don't usually carry that workload or even break down. Well, yoga helps prevent that from happening and also helps your body recover faster and loosen those tight areas. Moreover, through yoga, your balance and posture will improve and back issues will be assisted.

There are different types of yoga -- 11 or more distinct styles practiced in the U.S. alone. If you're into running long miles, go for the longer-pose Yin yoga sessions, as your body certainly needs an active break. Yin yoga poses are often up to two minutes long, so the focus in on rejuvination and lengthening muscles. If your running workload is more on the light side or you want some hard work during your offseason, you can go ahead and try some aerobically challenging, energetic yoga workouts, such as Vinyasa or Ashtanga.

Pilates benefits for runners

Because Pilates focuses on highly-controlled movements, it can give runners the benefit coordination, alignment, strength, and balance, a nice contrast from the repetitive nature of endurance training. Pilates is wonderful for strengthening your core, pelvis, and back, together with increasing your range of movement, flexibility, and strength. It works on making your main muscle areas stronger and, as long as you'll do it right, you'll really feel that rewarding burn. By doing Pilates on a regular basis, you'll enjoy an enhanced posture; this kind of workout makes you very aware of the way you run, stand, sit, and walk. And your stronger core that supports a straighter spine, you'll be surprised about your new, flawless running form. All the benefits of Pilates decrease your injury risk, especially when you start stacking up the miles.

Maybe you've noticed that many runners tend to breathe from their chest, particularly when picking up the pace. And we all know that deep, abdominal breathing is actually the correct way of doing it. Luckily, Pilates helps you improve the breathing pattern as well as your running rhythm.

When you often run, your knees can take a hammering. But if you include some Pilates into your training, you'll have your hip abductors and quads strengthened, which means great support to your hips and knees when you run. By making several areas of your body stronger, injuries are preventer easier and running power becomes greater. Awesome joints and muscles flexibility is another thing you'll enjoy after a few Pilates sessions.

Where To Find Yoga and Pilates

If you are interested in adopting yoga and Pilates into your workouts, but not quite sure where to go, you shouldn't have to look very hard. Both are offered in a multitude of places, and sometimes you can even take advantage of coaching without even leaving your house.

Here are a few good places to find yoga and Pilates.

- Gym or Health Club. Most health clubs have a full lineup of both yoga and Pilates classes. If you are already a health club member, there is a good chance that some level of class attendance is already included in your monthly membership. Be sure that the type of class is compatible with what you are looking for. In other words, don't show up at a hot yoga class if what you really want is a Vinyasa class.

- Boutique Gym. Many boutique gyms or shops specialize in either yoga or Pilates. You can buy a package of classes, or often pay by-the-time. The good thing about these shops is that the owner is often the instructor, and the quality of instruction is excellent. The bad thing is that this is almost always going to be the most expensive option.

- Online Streaming or Downloads. Streaming yoga classes can definitely be done online, both in free and subscription services. It is obviously a very convenient and cost-effective way to get your fix. You lose a bit, however, by not having in instructor there to watch and correct your movements and poses. Pilates is harder to do via video stream because special equipment is usually needed.

- DVDs. Many coaches and instructors offer DVDs which can be purchases and played at home. While DVDs are no longer the place where instructors are putting their best content, it can be a better option for people who live in areas with limited internet bandwidth.

You are now halfway done with this book, and hopefully you have already learned a few tips and lessons that you can begin to apply immediately!

If you are finding this information valuable, please consider leaving a review on Amazon. Your review will help others just like you make an informed buying decision, and I would personally be grateful if you chose to leave one!

Now, on with Chapter 12........

12. Incorporate Strength Training

In a meta-analysis of the effect of strength training on running, the National Institute of Health found that doing strength-training exercises 2-3 times per week has a demonstrated ability to improve the running economy -- the ability to run at velocity while consuming less oxygen -- in people who run middle and long distances.

Combining running (which is a cardio workout) with strength training is extremely beneficial to those of you who want to achieve faster times and avoid injuries. Running improves circulation and increases lung capacity, thus enhancing the intake of blood and oxygen delivered to your muscles; this, in turn, will be required for performing strength exercises. Doing strength training at least once a week, but ideally two or three times a week, not only increases muscle mass but also improves strength and resistance; it even plays a key role in burning fat.

Strength training has several effects on your running. First, it primes the pump which is the neuromuscular reflexes of your body structures. This happens before you even touch the ground with your feet when you run. So as you come in and you're about to land on your foot, your body will already pre-empting what's about to happen. Strength training improves those neuromuscular reflexes. Thus, when you land and strike the ground, a nicely orchestrated set of muscle activations occur before the other muscles propel you off to your next step. Therefore, strength training helps to prime your muscles and make the reflexes more efficient.

Another great thing about strength training is that it can reduce the risk of injury. This comes as a result of the muscle's enhanced power and efficiency to absorb the ground reaction forces that are shunted back up your legs as you land on them when you run. Hence, the stronger and more engaged your muscles are as you land, the fewer chances there are that these ground reaction forces to be harmful, overload your body, and cause injuries.

Strength exercises make you, as a runner, more efficient. This means that for a given speed of running you're able to run faster and for longer for the same energy costs. Strength training builds endurance in key muscles that will stabilize your body. As a result, you'll have better efficiency through your running technique.

Which Exercises Should I Do?

If you're more of a distance runner, focus on strengthening your muscles and keeping a slow-twitch muscle fiber that is aerobic, has nice endurance, and steady power. You can use bodyweight strength movements and core stabilizing exercises such as planks and leg raises. If you're a short distance runner, compound strength movements are your best friends. You can do anything that involves more than one joint: squats, deadlifts, bench presses, and so on.

A great exercise for all runners is the glute bridge which will help you fire those glutes and take less pressure off your quads and calf muscles. Lateral band walks are also amazing because you can adjust where you put the band on your leg: below the knee is the most challenging and all the way to your ankle is the easiest. This exercise works on your lateral movements, helping you improve hip stability, knee stability, and glute activation.

Core stability is very important when it comes to running; one of the best exercises to work on it is the side plank (hold it for 30+ seconds each side). Lateral lunges are wonderful for working those lateral muscles.

If you have access to weights, a couple exercises that are go-to for functional strength (you aren't trying to build your beach biceps here) are:

- Bent Over Row. Great for your upper and lower back, core, glutes, and hamstrings. Bend over at about 45-60 degrees, and pull either dumbbells or a barbell up to your chest from the floor while keeping the rest of your body still.

- Dead Lift. A great overall lift that requires you to have total control of your hips, core, and pelvis. The dead lift is the lift you often see power lifters do, where they simple grab on to a barbell that is on the floor, and with bent knees and a straight back, lift the bar up to their pelvis areas while standing straight up. Works the entire body, but especially the quads, hamstrings, glutes, back, and shoulders.

13. Think about your nutrition plan

Eating is one of the pleasures of life, right up there with running. Our body needs a combination of macronutrients in varying proportions in order to work at its full speed. On any given day, approximately 50 - 60% of calories must come from carbohydrates, up to 30% from healthy fats and about 10 - 20% from protein. But we also need some other protective elements such as vitamins or minerals. Of course, hydration is very important, too. A balanced diet requires regular significant fluid consumption, essential during running.

Keep in mind that all you put into your body (food, liquids, nutritional supplements) have to fulfil several roles simultaneously:

- Fuel - here we're talking about calories from certain macronutrients (lipids, carbs, proteins).

- Protection - this is ensured by macronutrients (vitamins, minerals), fiber, and antioxidants.

- Thermoregulation - here we have to mention water, which, among other benefits, also normalizes our bodies' temperature.

- Maintenance - once again, proteins, along with other essential amino acids, play a decisive role in the permanent tissue regeneration.

A runner can be compared to a limited edition racing car. In order to always achieve great results, it needs the best fuel. Well, in your case, food, with all its awesome nutrients, is exactly the fuel that helps with:

- Muscle tissues development

- Strengthening the bones

- Keeping your joints healthy

- Maintaining your physical fitness

- Energizing the body

- Optimizing stress resistance

- Fighting against stress-related nutrient deficiencies.

Carbohydrates are a primary source of fuel for runners and have to make about 50% to 60% of your diet. This percentage will ensure that you achieve peak performance levels and will also sugar levels in control. Some sources of complex carbohydrates include oatmeal, bran, whole grain bread, brown rice, and whole wheat pasta.

After an intense running session, you need to ensure your lean muscle tissue recovery and **proteins** are just right for that. They not only support your tissue recovery but also help preserve your lean muscles. Lean protein sources include fish, chicken, tofu, and low-fat dairy products.

Consuming a fair amount of **healthy fats** can improve satiety with each meal, thereby preventing hunger pangs between meals. Healthy fats also support digestion as well as protect your muscles and joints from excess damage. Omega 3 and omega 6 are essential fatty acids found in olive oil, fatty fish, nuts, and seeds.

Even if **vitamins** are not the source of energy for runners, they should still be included in your nutrition plan. Running can lead to the formation of certain compounds called free radicals; unfortunately, they aren't very beneficial to your cells. Vitamins A, C and E are antioxidants that neutralize these free radicals. Therefore, make sure that your diet is rich in vitamins.

When talking about **minerals**, calcium, iron, sodium, and other electrolytes are very beneficial to each and every runner. Calcium helps prevent osteoporosis and fractures, which is why a calcium-rich nutrition is very important for runners. You can take care of your daily calcium intake by consuming low-fat dairy products, calcium-rich beverages, eggs, and beans. Iron plays a key role in cell oxygenation. Iron deficiency can lead to weight loss and fatigue, especially during training. During runtimes, while sweating, you lose small amounts of sodium and other electrolytes. With proper nutrition, they will restore. There are several sports drinks on the market that are rich in electrolytes. Also, you can go for salty snacks, but make sure you choose a healthy product.

As far as **supplements** are concerned, as their name indicates, they only supplement (never entirely provide) a healthy and balanced nutrition that you need to achieve your top performance level.

I wrote another book on the topic of using diet to get more out of your workouts. Like this book, it includes a number of tips and habits that are easy to incorporate. Fit Foods can be found on Amazon.

14. Get plenty of quality rest and sleep

Getting enough sleep and rest is not just important for your physical health, but also for your mental health, quality of life, and your safety. Therefore, when you're running, it's essential to never neglect this aspect.

Not sleeping and resting enough for a period of time can set off all sorts of different hormonal shifts in your body, raise your heart rate, make you feel nervous and anxious, increase your cortisol levels, thus your stress. Plus, keep in mind the human growth hormone is secreted during deep sleep; the less sleep you get, the lower your levels and the slower your recovery will be. Hence, getting that deep sleep will help you get rid of those aches and pains and improve your muscles' ability to store glycogen. Being sleep and rest deprived doesn't just make you tired; it can make you jittery, achy, injury-prone, and grumpy.

Sleep is actually part of your workout cycle, because muscles develop during rest and not during physical exercise. The effort is just the stimulus of growth, but muscle hypertrophy occurs when the muscle is no longer 'used', which happens especially when you sleep. And because your muscles are really important for running results, those who don't sleep enough for a while will certainly notice their performance stagnating or even going downhill. The motor skills, coordination skills, and strength will get altered. In other words, they'll notice that they can't run like they want to; they'll get tired much faster, and won't be able to focus.

A study by the U.S. National Institute of Health (NIH) demonstrated that there is a strong correlation between healthy sleep habits and competitive performance in athletes. As sleep was comprimised, decreases in performance levels and incrases in injuries were noted.

All of the information we talked about above make it pretty obvious that sleep and rest are key to feeling great on a daily basis and enhancing your running performance. A great idea for achieving the benefits we've just mentioned is to start sleep loading. This means that during your training weeks you have to accumulate lots and lots of good extra sleep. Even if we're talking about an extra half hour, that's really going to help. However, try to treat yourself with a couple of extra hours, if your schedule allows you.

Although there are significant differences between people (some sleep 6 hours and feel perfectly rest, while others need 10 hours of sleep), an average of 7 to 8 hours per night is recommended for most individuals. Try waking up at the same time every morning (even during weekends). Also, try going to bed at the same time each evening. A regular sleeping schedule will make your running training as effective as possible. Napping during the day isn't mandatory, so if you don't feel tired, don't force yourself to sleep.

Many studies found that exercising 3-4 hours before bedtime alters sleep. So be careful when planning your running sessions. It's also known that when exercise is performed in early afternoon improves the depth of sleep.

Caffeine, tea, and supplements with neurostimulating properties should be avoided 4-6 hours before bedtime. While alcohol is known to make us drowsy at first, it negatively affects the last cycle of sleep even if it's consumed in small amounts.

The place where you sleep should be as comfortable and cozy as possible. Extreme temperatures, light and noise should be avoided. Noise is the most common problem, which sometimes can't be controlled; its negative impact on sleep can, however, be reduced using a device that masks the noise such as a fan.

If you have difficulty "turning your mind off" at bedtime, consider a melatonin supplement. It can create drowsiness and help with your first couple hours of sleep, but doesn't tend to leave grogginess the next day. 1mg is a lite dose, while 10mg is a heavier dose. If you sense that your sleep quality is poor on a consistent basis, see your doctor. Many common sleep issues, such as sleep apnea, can be resolved with a little medical intervention.

15. Get new shoes every 300 miles

Changing your pair of running shoes has to be taken very seriously, and too many runners blow it off. Not changing your shoes often enough is a common way to get injured, and it can negatively impact your performance. You wear special running footwear to protect your beloved feet from all the surfaces you constantly run on and to maintain an optimal function of your joints and muscles. As shoes are wearing out, their form, support, and grip decrease.

Over time, your shoes will get thinner and the cushioning's midsole layer will diminish. Even if your body is a master at adapting, eventually, when the midsole becomes very thin, your running gait has to comprimise in order to compensate for the lack of support. It can lead to injury; changing your shoes before they get to this stage is essential.

In most cases, running shoes should be changed every 300 miles. Some runner, especially those who are lighter weight and have no known injury or soreness issues, may be able to go as high as 500 miles, but for other runners 500 will be pushing past the point of risk. In order to know when it's time to transition to a new pair, get an app or use your GPS system that will track the mileage on your running shoes. By the time you have 300 miles of use on a running shoe, the midsection layer of that shoe's sole is typically about 40% worn out.

Another easy hack that many runners use is to write the first date of use on the new shoe. Use a sharpie and write it in a place that will not easily get worn off. Then, you can at least have a rough idea of how many miles are probably on your shoe by calculating your typically weekly mileage.

Signs that your running shoes are worn out

- An important sign indicating that your shoes need to be changed is feeling more tired and fatigued than you should be even though you do the same loop every day.

- Struggling with sore, tired calves, little, small aches and pains in your knee, your lower back, or your hips, that tend to go away very shortly after a run is another sign hinting that your shoes need to be changed.

- Take a look at the bottom of your shoe, specifically at the area underneath the ball of the foot. If it's really soft, spongy, and squishy, then it's really the time for a new pair of shoes. This cushion should be firm and responsive.

- If you see distress lines, wrinkles, or discolorations all the way through the midsole and the midsole is pretty compressed, go for new running shoes as soon as possible.

Test if your footwear is worn out

- Squeeze the midfoot and then the heel; you should feel a slight amount of 'give' and then a little pushback as you let go. If it feels dead or there's no return at all, the cushioning is gone, so it's time to part with your shoes.

- Fold the midsole by pushing the toe towards the heel. This shouldn't be easy to do, but if your shoe folds in half, then the midsole is worn out.

- Perform a twist test. Move the front of the shoe in a different direction to the heel. Motion control is vital in running shoes because it controls your foot as it hits the ground. Thus, you shouldn't be able to twist your shoes. If however your shoe easily rings out, it's another sign that the midsole is worn out.

How to choose your running shoes

There are some basic rules to choose the pair of running shoes that will keep you away from injuries and help you increase your performance.

Choose a high-quality pair of running shoes

Before you buy a pair of shoes, take some time to research and find out what equipment is best for your running technique and level, what top-notch footwear is available on the market, which are the products that are highly appreciated by fellow runners. A good pair of shoes is extremely important, whether you are a beginner or a seasoned runner. You need protection for your muscles, joints, and ligaments, as well as need shoes that offer great shock absorption, good motion control, flexibility, and durability.

Wearing unsuitable shoes is one of the main causes of injury in runners. You have to make sure that your running shoes offer optimal support and damping to prevent damage to the ligaments, tendons, and joints. Your footwear must match the shape of your sole and your running style.

Determine your foot pronation

Even if it looks simple, running is a complex biomechanical process. Generally, when you run, first you touch the ground with the outside of your heel so that the leg rises from the ground and pushes the heel to move forward. This process is called pronation. An exaggerated pronation movement can cause injuries, especially in the lower leg and knee. Also, a poor pronation can lead to trauma.

Pronation is influenced by the shape of your sole, and to find out where you fit, it's enough to examine the footprint you leave on a flat surface. If your footprint is very full and it doesn't show an arch, then you have a foot with narrow, flat arch. Instead, a very thin and curved footprint, with a very pronounced heel, means you have a high arch. An intermediate shape means a normal arch.

- If your foot is flat, then you have an exaggerated pronation movement.

- If your foot has a high arch, then your pronation movement is insufficient.

- If your foot has a normal shape, then your pronation movement is normal.

Once you've identified the shape of your foot and your pronation, you can choose the suitable running shoes. The footwear's shape is one of the most important aspects to consider when opting for a new pair.

- If your pronation movement is exaggerated, go for straight lasted shoes.

- If your pronation movement is insufficient, choose curved last running shoes.

- If your pronation movement is normal, semi-curved last running shoes should be perfect for you.

When in doubt, go to a running store to buy your shoes. Not a generic all-purpose sporting goods store in the mall, but an actual running store. The staff there work with runners of all levels, and can help you match the right shoe with your needs and running style. Be sure you explain to them any soreness or injury you have experience. There is a strong chance they can help you correct that problem with the right shoe, perhaps one you have never considered before.

Finally, once you find a shoe that makes your knees and your body happy and feels good, stick with it. Most runners use the exact same model of shoe for years on end, just getting a new pair ever 300-500 miles. The only time you really need to change is when your body changes and a new type of support is called for.

16. Use a foam roller

When it comes to staying healthy, most endurance runners, triathletes, and other active folks will tell you that their secret weapon is a simple piece of foam that costs about $20: A foam roller.

Foam rolling is very important for runners in terms of recovery and injury prevention. A foam roller acts as a way for you to massage yourself and breaks down the adhesions between the muscles. If your muscles are really sore and stiff, foam rolling will bring blood flow to that area in order to break up the myofascial adhesions between the muscles, thus speeding up the recovery process. It also tends to reduce delayed onset muscle soreness (DOMS) in many runners, the syndrome that makes an athlete sore a day or more after exercise. DOMS is called "muscle fever", and my personal experience is that foam rolling after a workout can have profound reductions in its effect.

Regular foam rolling will help relieve some of the stresses that build up in your muscles and joints and prevent injuries from happening. When it comes to the foam roller, the big thing to remember is that consistency is your friend. The more often you do it the more effective it is and the healthier you'll stay as a runner. So by regularly taking care of your muscles, you're going to keep running for longer, you'll not be as likely to deal with injuries, and you're just going to feel better.

Foam roller exercises

IT Band. Many runners are first introduced to a foam roller because of an IT Band issue. Nothing can work a knot out of the IT Band like a good hunk of foam. Sit with your hand bracing your body behind you, and place the roller under one of your thighs, on the outer side. Cross your legs to give the side on the roller the full weight. Then, beginning moving back and forth on top of the roller, rolling the area from your hip down to the side of your knee. Do it until you feel your thigh "release", which will happen. Once you hit the key trigger point, you will know it. This exercise can be a bit painful, but in a good way.

Calves. As a runner, you use your calves a lot, therefore this is a significant area to focus on. Place the roller underneath the middle of your calves, put both legs on the roller, keep your hands flat on the floor behind you and then pick your hips off the floor. Start rolling slowly from below your knees (very top of your calves) to just above your ankles (very bottom your calves). Do that until you locate the trigger points or knots in your muscles. Once you've located the trigger points, pause for approximately 20 seconds and press down on those trigger points. If you identify trigger points in only one leg, then take the other leg and put it on top for some added pressure. Pause, take some deep breaths and let the muscle ease out. After those 20 pause seconds have passed, start doing some cross friction rotations. Rotate your legs from left to right in order to get that cross friction on the roller. Do about 5 - 10 slow rotations.

Quads. Flip over, place the roller at about the middle of your quads, go down into a kind of a plank position, but with your quads on the foam roller. Keep your hands locked in a triangle position for good stability. Do 30 seconds of slow rolling until you locate the trigger points. Once you've located a trigger point, stand still for 20 seconds, press down, and let your muscles ease them out. After that, move on and do 5 - 10 cross friction rotations: rotate to the left and to the right.

Hamstrings. Place your roller underneath the middle of your hamstrings, keep your hands flat on the floor behind you and pick your hips off the floor. This is actually very similar to the calves exercise position. Roll slowly to just above the knees and then in the opposite direction to just below the bottom of your glutes. Do this for 30 seconds, slowly, until you locate your trigger points. Once you've located a trigger point, pause for 20 seconds, pressing down and allowing the muscle tension to ease off, the blood flow to get back to where it needs to be, and those essential nutrients to repair the muscle tissues. After that, do 5 - 10 cross friction rotations.

Adductors. Flip over, use your arms to support your body, put the foam roller at a 45-degree angle, place the adductor on it and slowly roll your muscle over until you locate a trigger point. Once your trigger point is identified, pause for 20 seconds; hold your leg down against the roller, in order for the muscle tension to release. Then, do 5 - 10 cross friction rotations: bring your leg up and then bring it down. Repeat the exact same thing for your other leg.

Glutes. Sit straight on top of the roller, keep your hands behind you, and slowly roll from just above where the hamstrings meet the glutes to your lower back, looking for trigger points. Do that until you find a trigger point, and then pause for 20 seconds, holding on to it. After that, do 5 - 10 cross friction rotations: keep your feet flat on the ground and roll your knees from one side to another.

Piriformis. Sit on the roller, keep one hand behind you, place one leg directly on top of the other knee, and slightly rotate towards the side of the muscle you're massaging. Roll slowly, find a tense spot, and pause on that section for 20 seconds, allowing your muscle to release the tension. Once the pause is over, perform 5 - 10 cross friction rotations by lifting the knee up and down.

17. Incorporate interval training

Interval training is a simple method of training that focuses on alternating between running at a fast pace and running at a slower pace. It helps you improve your speed and endurance. In order to do interval training, you first need to know your MAS (Maximal Aerobic Speed).

The best intervals will make you work quite hard during the short, hard burst, and let you rest -- but not for enough time to fully recover. That is the magic of an interval session. You are getting some nice, hard, intense work, but also giving yourself practice recovering as well.

Here's how you find out and use your MAS

The maximum aerobic speed (MAS) can help you set measurable aims during your training so that you stay healthy whilst running. Your MAS means the speed at which you run when your oxygen intake is at its maximum. It matches your cardiovascular capacities and the more the more oxygen your body is able to take in, the higher your MAS and the greater your fitness capacity. If you know your MAS, you'll be able to set running goals that are consistent with your physical abilities. Thus, you'll avoid pushing yourself too far. Here's a quick, simple exercise to find out your MAS: warm-up and run for about 6 minutes as far as you can. Keep your speed as steady as possible. After that, measure the distance you ran during those 6 minutes and divide it to 100 in order to get your speed in kilometers per hour. This number is your MAS. The thing is that you can only run for a few minutes at your full MAS; for longer physical efforts, train to run at 80% to 90% of your MAS. You will then be able to maintain your speed for the duration of your run.

Now, back to interval training

We're going to talk about two types of interval training exercises: the short interval and the long interval.

- Short interval training helps you enhance your MAS. Run at 100% of your MAS for about 30 seconds and then jog for another 30 seconds in order to recover. Repeat this exercise 10 times.

- Long interval training helps you enhance your ability to maintain your speed close to your MAS for a long period of time. Run at 90% of your MAS for about 0.7 miles and then jog for 0.25 miles in order to recover. Perform this exercise 3 times.

High-Intensity Interval Training (HIIT) for faster times

HIIT consists of repeated bouts of high-intensity exercise (performed at close to 100% maximal oxygen intake - VO2max) interspersed with short recovery periods. It's considered one of the most effective exercise forms for improving physical performance. HIIT is thought to increase your skeletal muscle's ability to buffer hydrogen ions, increase your anaerobic capacity, and increase your motor unit activation. So, by integrating some HIIT training into your workout routine, you'll be able to get those faster times. Some ideas are to use a 1:1 ratio (30 seconds on, 30 seconds off), 1:2 ratio (30 seconds on 1 minute off), a 2:1 ratio (30 seconds on, 15 seconds off), or you can go Tabata style (20 seconds on, 10 seconds off).

The great thing about interval training is that you can get a very high-quality workout in just a short amount of time. I included several additional interval workouts in my 30-minute workout guide, *30 Essential Running Workouts, 30 Minutes or Less* (here on Amazon).

18. Shorten your stride

Do you know those runs where you feel like you're floating on the ground and you could go forever? Sounds awesome, doesn't it? The great news is that through technique and stride, you can duplicate that. Being in control of your stride will allow you to increase your endurance, speed, and keep far away from injuries.

A lot of newbies think that the best runners would get further with every single step, but that is not entirely true. Bigger is not always better and unfortunately, a lot of folks have the tendency to overstride. You actually want to have a shorter step and you want your feet to land under your body; that's going to keep you balanced. The other aspect you want to consider is low-impact. You don't want your feet landing hard, waste loads of energy, and add force to your landing. Your landings have to be light and graceful.

Talking about strides, there was a study from the University of Wisconsin (2010) which reported that shorter strides can have several benefits. According to this study, the runners who decreased their stride length bounced less, managed to land closer to their mass center, as well as had lower braking forces when they hit the ground. Shorter strides allowed the runner's knee to work less while absorbing energy and high-cadence allowed the runner's hip to work less. A shorter stride also allowed the runner's knee do less bending during the stance; plus, it decreased several hip motions.

We've just talked about cadence, and there are some important things every runner should know. First, improving your cadence (stride rate) can help you prevent overstriding. Your running cadence is the number of times your feet strike the ground in a one-minute time frame. It's essential to have a good, efficient stride because that helps promote a nice mid-foot strike, mid-foot landing, reduces your heel strike, and ultimately helps you reduce the injury risk. There are a few different ways you can really start to improve your cadence. For example:

- Find a nice, gradual downhill slope where you can do short strides. Go down the hill five to ten times and focus on getting a quick turnover while holding a good form. Do this every single week.

- Run with a metronome app. This is a great way to start understanding how running at a higher cadence feels like. There are lots of apps you can find out there; choose one and set whatever cadence you want.

- Jump up the treadmill, set it at a fairly quick speed, somewhere a bit faster than you easy run, and start to run along with that. Focus on short, quick strides and then try taking long, slow strides. You'll notice the difference between those two and how they feel like. The short, quick turnover is what you're looking for, and by alternating strides, you'll understand that a lot of times when trying to run faster, we tend to overstride. So, by being aware of that, and knowing how overstriding feels like, you'll be able to avoid it.

19. Become a mid-foot striker

The mid-foot strike is a new concept that's gained lots of popularity in the recent years. Its most common definition is running with your forefoot and your heel striking the ground at the same time. The mid-foot strike is thought to decrease injury risk as well as improve your running efficiency.

Compared to the heel strike, the mid-foot strike involves lower impact forces. And, if you focus on gradually increasing training with this running form while working on the strength and flexibility of your calves and Achilles tendons, you can lessen the stress on these muscles and tendons. Also, mid-foot landing is great for avoiding overstriding, which is very common in heel-first foot strikers.

In order to become a mid-foot striker, begin with building up some strength in your Achilles tendons and calves. Gradually, start doing some of your fast tempo runs and interval training landing on the mid-foot. Take your time, the change won't happen overnight. But a good way to motivate yourself is constantly tracking your progress.

It's important to know that your arms are an essential element of flawless biomechanics for the mid-foot technique. When you're mid-foot running, your arms play three main roles:

- They help you maintain the right cadence. A mid-foot strike asks for keeping a certain cadence. Otherwise, your lower leg's elastic recoil will no longer work. Especially if you're just starting to practice the mid-food technique, your arms will help you maintain your cadence.

- They help to optimize the use of the 'spinal engine'. The mid-foot strike seeks to maximize the use of your spinal engine. The 'engine' we're talking about runs by using natural twist mechanisms which occur in your upper body.

- They help you perform a more powerful stride. By pulling your arms, you will increase your stride's power. As a mid-foot striker, you have to emphasize the pulling of the arm behind you by simply lifting your elbow. When you arm swings back in front of you, your elbow should barely go ahead of the trunk.

Also regarding strikes, there are some common mistakes you need to avoid:

- Don't force a toe strike. That can cause plenty of tension in other areas of your lower legs. Thus, don't be too far on your feet's balls.

- Avoid heel striking. It can increase your risk of getting injured because of the high impact associated with it. Heel pain, lower leg pain, Achilles injury, broken hip femur, and low back pain are just some of the injuries you can struggle with due to heel striking, so try staying far away from it.

20. Open your hips with exercises

If you want to run faster, opening your hips will help you significantly. Tight hip flexors have a domino effect on your running. They cause your glutes to be underused, and can shift your stride to be just a bit misaligned. All of the issues can then cause other problems, which in turn create more injuries. The best policy is to keep your flexors nice and loose.

There are some exercises that will make it easier for you to open your hips. The moves listed below are awesome for hip mobility, but also if you struggle with glute pain or hip flexor flunk.

1. **Single leg glute bridge.** Lay down on the floor, relax your upper body, place your arms to the side, bend your knees, and tighten up your abdominal area. Lift up your hips until your hips, knees, and shoulders are in line. Straighten out one leg, hold that for a second, bring the leg back, and go back down. Relax for a moment and repeat with the other leg.

Make sure that your movement is controlled, smooth, with a good stop at the end position. This exercise has a light to medium intensity and it targets hip stability, the core, and the glutes. All of this will help when it relates to running. Perform one set of 5 repetitions on each leg.

2. **Donkey kicks.** Start off with a four-point position: knees underneath your hips, hands underneath your shoulders, you're in a straight line when it relates to hip, shoulders, and head. Tighten the abdominal area. Lift one leg up while keeping the knee bent at 90 degrees. Once your knee is in line with your hip, hold for a second, then come back down and switch legs. The movement

should be smooth and controlled, with a good stop at the top position.

The intensity of this exercise is more on the light side, but besides hips, you're targeting your core, glutes, and hamstrings: important areas when it comes to getting stronger, increase running performance, and prevent injuries. Perform one set of 5 repetitions on each leg.

3. **Side-lying hip abduction.** Lay down on your side with one arm overhead, resting your head on your arm. Slightly bend your knees to prevent rocking forward and back. Tighten up your abs and lift your top leg up (to a 30-45 degrees angle), hold for one second, and then bring it back down. Relax and repeat. Again, you should maintain a controlled, smooth movement with a good stop at the top position.

This exercise has a light intensity. Its purpose is to target the outer hip, the core, the abdominal area, and the gluteus medius. The movement will help you improve stability and support. Thus, when you'll run, you'll be able to prevent your hips from rocking too much side to side, which would put unnecessary stress to the hips and knees. Perform one set of 5 repetitions on each side.

4. **Butt-Up Squats.** We like the butt up squat, and it is just like it sounds. You go into a squatting position with your legs a bit further than shoulder-width apart. Have your thighs pretty close to 90 degrees parallel to the ground. Then, simply begin to pulse your glutes up and down, never standing straight up, but never sitting all the way down either. Do this for about 30 seconds and rest. Your quads should be burning, and your hips will gradually begin to open up.

Other wonderful hip opening exercises you can try are bird dogs and lunge to knee drives.

21. Stretch!

We saved the best for last. If there was only one tip we could tell a runner to help them stay healthier and get faster, it would be to stretch. Stretch before workouts, after workouts, and even on non-workout days.

Stretching exercises, in their basic form, are natural and instinctive movements. You certainly do such exercises in the morning after waking up or after a long period of inactivity. As a form of movement, stretching involves stretching a particular muscle or group of muscles to the maximum size.

What's the point of stretching? Well, stretching is one of the best preventative measures to muscle tightness. Essentially, stretching helps your muscle fibers to release more easily. Plus, it decreases your chances to get any type of injuries.

Stretching increases the blood and nutrient flow to your cartilages and muscles. At the same time, a good blood circulation removes residuals in your body and helps recover quickly from injuries.

As we age, our muscles tend to atrophy, restricting flexibility. This leads to low mobility, slow movements, ligament dislocations and tissue injuries. Stretching exercises are extremely effective in improving mobility and flexibility.

Not to mention that stretching can improve and even correct a faulty posture. When stretching, the tension from your muscles is released. Muscle tension accumulation is responsible for muscle rigidity, one of the most common causes of faulty posture. Stretching movements help to properly align the spine, improving the posture while eliminating the back pain or discomfort.

Should you stretch before or after your running?

The short answer is both. But wait, there's something you should know. There's actually a difference between the type of stretching you should do before and after running. Before running you need to do dynamic stretches, while after running you need to do static stretches.

A dynamic stretch is where you're moving during the stretch, for example, a leg swing. A static stretch is where you're simply holding a stretch, for example, a bent-knee calf stretch. Dynamic stretching is meant to give you mobility to loosen up your muscles. Therefore, you'll be ready to go out and run. Static stretching is meant to give you a really deep stretch into your muscles. Thus, you'll be able to return the elasticity to your muscles after you're done with your run. It's basically a one-two combination that is designed to keep your muscles nice, flexible, elastic, and strong for your running.

Conclusion - And a Favor

Whether you're a newbie or an experienced runner, you certainly take running pretty seriously. However, it's important to always keep a tiny dose of auto-irony and humor at hand and use it whenever you're dealing with tough moments during your training or races. Make the best of your running time, as every single moment is unique.

If you enjoyed this book, or found it useful, please consider leaving a review on Amazon. Your review is incredibly important to me, and will help other runners decide if this is a good book for them to consider.

Regardless of the reasons you run, we hope that this guide will help you achieve your goals and fulfil a dream that many of us have, yet few of us express it: to keep running and enjoy it all our lives. More, faster, without pain and without injuries. Happy running!

FURTHER READING

My other books can also be found on Amazon, and may help provide additional ideas and perspective.

30 Essential Running Workouts, 30 Minutes or Less. Time-strapped? This book provides 30 excellent running and cross-training workouts that help you make the most of your training time.

Fit Foods: 21 Nutrition Rules for Getting More From Your Training, Runs, and Workouts. Nutrition is a secret weapon of anyone who is training or trying to get more fit. This guide breaks it down in laymen's terms.

Your First Triathlon Guide: 100 Days to Your First Triathlon. For total body conditioning, and a great balance of cardio and muscular fitness, there is no better sport than triathlon. I give you the step-by-step on how you can enjoy the sport.

Finally, my email subscribers are the first to hear about the best gear and equipment deals, as well as new content that might be helpful. I don't send many emails, so don't worry – I won't clutter your inbox! You can sign up here.

Made in the USA
Middletown, DE
06 September 2020